Things My Daddy Said

(AN AUTOBIOGRAPHICAL BOOK OF VALUABLE LIFE PRINCIPLES or maybe WISDOM PERSONIFIED)

Paulette Pierce Holloway

STUDIO OF BOOKS
THE SPACE FOR YOUR MESSAGE

Studio of Books LLC
5900 Balcones Drive Suite 100
Austin, Texas 78731
www.studioofbooks.org
Hotline: (254) 800-1183

Ordering Information:
Special discounts are available on quantity purchases by corporations, associations, and others. For details, contact the publisher at the address above.

Printed in the United States of America.

ISBN-13: Softcover   978-1-964148-05-2
          eBook   978-1-964148-06-9

Library of Congress Control Number: 2024906614

Dedication

This book is dedicated to the memory of my amazing parents, Charlie Lee Pierce and Zetta Mae Washington Pierce, and my siblings, John, Patricia, Jeffrey (Deceased), and Pamela. To God be the Glory!!

Contents

Introduction

I have been trying to figure out life for as long as I can remember. I asked questions about why people acted the way they did, why there was injustice, why I looked different, and so on. My Daddy was usually the recipient of my questions, and he had a way of putting things together on such an easy-to-understand level that I was motivated to keep asking. He passed away in 1995 at age 68. I was 43 years old back then, and believe it or not, I am still quoting any one of those many sayings he would seemingly effortlessly drop on me when I made an inquiry if I needed some advice or if he was just in a talking mood. Being reflective as I think about him and trying to give better insight into who he was, I might compare him to, let's say, Ben Franklin because, to me, he was full of adages. Or if I compared him to the scriptures, I would say maybe even like Christ because he was full of parables. Either way, he was, to me, full of wisdom that influenced my childhood and into my adult life. His wisdom was awe-inspiring as I think back on things, awe-inspiring because my dad had a 7th-grade education and never really mastered the reading and writing skills that one would have expected (or supposed) that he possessed. He was looked up to by most people that he met and had a commanding way about him that got him into some very unlikely places. He was a visionary and a masterful manipulator of negative circumstances, always believing that there was more than one right answer. One example of the proof of that philosophy was when, back in 1957, he and our mom purchased a business that was initially being denied them because of their race. Racism and segregation were very prevalent in rural Virginia in those days, yet that mindset of overcoming odds allowed them to purchase and own that business for more than 20 years until, as they aged, they decided to sell. That mindset also influenced us in our developmental years, to believe that we could achieve most anything we set our minds to. The stories are too numerous to include in this book to support that last statement, but I know if my older sister were helping me write this, she, too, could attest to these and so many more nuggets that we gleaned from our dad.

This book is being written partly because I have had people literally from all over the world tell me I should write down the things that I have shared with them that my Daddy said. I told a "My Daddy used to say" story in Rwanda, East Africa, that motivated awe and inspiration, and even generated pleading to write it down for others to benefit from it. The young man who was the recipient of the story literally begged me to publish it, so I have included it in this book. I also have several close friends who have prodded me over the years, insisting that I put all the sayings that I repeat that my Daddy said in writing. One of my dear friends, in particular, has been a champion (and agitator for the cause) for many years, as she lovingly refers to me as Virginia Peanut. My husband also has inspired me to write the book because he has gotten bombarded with so many of my various "Daddy sayings." He has made heart-felt comments, sorrowfully lamenting over the fact that he did not get the privilege to have known him. The other reason, and possibly the strongest that this book is being written, is because I woke up one morning with the idea so strong to write it that I actually had to grab the notepad by my bed and start itemizing the things that popped up in my mind as I remembered them. I had written twelve sayings within 15 minutes and realized that it could not be coincidental that I was having that experience. I surrendered to the fact that I needed to stop playing around with the idea and simply get it done.

Each of the chapters will come with a full story about how I happened to get that particular saying, piece of advice, or words of wisdom. The stories are from my everyday life and hopefully will be so easily relatable that, at best, they will give you a fresh perspective on navigating through situations that may occur in our lives. At the least, the stories will be entertaining and make it easy to laugh at yourself and your own parenting methods or childhood experiences. Some of the stories were born out of my pain, some out of my innocence, and some out of my day-to-day life struggles. Some of the stories will be much shorter than others simply because the experience only warranted a little bit of conversation. My hope is that at least one of them will resonate with you in a personal way and encourage you to smile, put things in perspective, and keep on growing.

My initial thought was to try to group the sayings into categories for a more cohesive flow, with heading divisions to introduce each category, but that became a challenge as I kept going, so I partially abandoned that notion. Instead, what I have done is group the chapters as closely as I can with similar concepts without making distinct divisions throughout the book. I can say that the first few chapters will be related to the importance of the commonsense use of finances. Others, as you will discover, will fall into categories of their own and will allow you to make up your own categories. My hope is that each chapter will in some way inspire you from the things my Daddy used to say.

To honor my mother, though this book highlights my Daddy, I want to make it very clear that in every way, my mother was blessed with her own amazing level of wisdom and contributed to a significant level of my being who I am. Her practical approach to life shaped the positive direction of our family and influenced so many of our decisions. As quiet as it's kept, who is to say that many of my Daddy's sayings didn't get birthed out of his relationship with our mom?

ALL YOUR MONEY IS IN YOUR CABINET

"Do not lay up for yourselves treasures on earth, where moth and rust destroy and where thieves break in and steal; 20 but lay up for yourselves treasures in heaven, where neither moth nor rust destroys and where thieves do not break in and steal."

Matthew 6:19-20

This saying is one of a two-part saying that will follow in the next chapter. This all came about one day in my early days of marriage when our family budget was meager, to say the least, even though I had a hard-working husband. It was one of those days when I had gone to the grocery store, and not knowing all the nutritional facts that are so important today, I had bought my stock of canned goods. I was tallying up my budget and quickly seeing that I had overspent by $20, causing me to go into a tailspin. While I was trying to figure out things on my own, my dad stopped by just to say hello and to check on his grandson. I was putting away the last of the groceries, so that caused our visit to take place in the kitchen. As I swallowed my pride and got my courage together (which, truthfully, I did not need to do), I asked Daddy if he would give me $20. (Now, of course, what you could not possibly know is that Daddy and I had a little trade secret. If I needed money that I knew I could pay back, I would ask for a loan, and conversely, if I needed money that I could not readily pay back, I asked for a gift. The request would sometimes sound like, "Daddy, could you loan me $50

and give me $20?" The amazing thing about that financial arrangement is that he always came through and in the manner that I requested. And interestingly, though he easily could have, he never volunteered to make it all a gift).

Now, moving on to the rest of the story. Before I was able to get the response that I wanted to get, that is, the cash in my hand, Daddy asked me a simple question. What I had not noticed was that as I was restocking my cabinets, he was surveying the contents of my cabinet shelves as he considered my request. Thoughtfully, he asked me what I had in my cabinet simply because the cabinet doors were still open from stocking my shelves. I thought the response was a little odd, but knowing our history, I wasn't remotely discouraged that he would honor my request. I looked over at my open cabinet doors, and I went about naming the items on the shelves. Before too long into the process, he interrupted me as I got to the several cans of the next item. I want to say that it was Carnation evaporated milk (my grandmother's favorite brand), but after all these years, I can't be positive. It might have been cans of creamed corn in that I bought them both often to make my corn pudding. Without giving it any thought, I remember proudly chiming out that there were four cans. Then he asked me that next thoughtful question. "How many cans did you need"? I responded that I really only needed one but quickly justified that they were on sale "4 for a dollar". So, the conversation progressed to "Do you need to use more than one can any time soon"? And, of course, I had to respond with a negative. My Dad looked at me very matter-of-factly and asked, "Would the store have sold you just one can? "And of course, I had to say yes, they would have. He thought about it a little more and added, "All your money is in your cabinet." His comment was so eye-opening that I had to sit down and really think about it. As the conversation continued, he went on to point out that a sale is only a good sale for you if you need to use the merchandise that you are buying.

That conversation caused me to think about other purchases I had made, especially in the category of food items, but it was not limited there. Sometimes, when you stock up on items, you don't use them before they expire, and, in those cases, did you really save any money?

Sometimes, you stock up on clothes either for yourself or your children, and the size you found at that great sale price becomes too small or outdated by the time you even remember you bought it. Again, did you really save any money?

Ultimately, my dad gave me the $20 that I requested (as I knew he would), but the gift came with so much more. I am so grateful that just that seemingly simple conversation that day so many years ago was one of those conversations that was the source of an impartation of wisdom that has guided my decisions over my life and has contributed mightily to my respect for good stewardship. My hope is that you, too, will be able to glean some valuable financial wisdom from that very seemingly simple question and the profound statement that followed.

IF IT GOES ON SALE ONCE, IT WILL GO ON SALE AGAIN

"Therefore, do not worry, saying, 'What shall we eat?' or 'What shall we drink?' or 'What shall we wear?' 32 For after all these things, the Gentiles seek. For your heavenly Father knows that you need all these things."

Matthew 6:31-32

One of the greatest challenges that a true shopper/consumer can face is the challenge of walking away from a sale. I have friends who buy things they don't need, can't use, can't wear, nor have anyone in mind to be the recipient of their good fortune. They just can't resist the sale. I am sure that I was once somewhat like that type of person, though not for frivolous reasons. My sales frenzies had to do more with trying to save money for fear of not having the money when I really needed that thing or calling myself a good steward because I was spending God's money wisely.

Well, as reflected in the previous chapter, one day, I had been grocery shopping, trying to stretch my few dollars as far as possible to feed my family, and when I was home and moving on to the next financial obligation, I discovered that I was $20 short. My Dad happened to stop by, and knowing our relationship, I decided to ask him for $20.

Daddy was quite consistent in his responses when I made a request in that they were always in the affirmative, but they also were usually accompanied by some kind of parable or thought-provoking. This time, it was in conjunction with the previous chapter's message. Once he had given me that little tidbit about my money being in my cabinet, he shared the concept of sales shopping. He said, in the form of a question, "You do know that if it goes on sale one time, it will go on sale again, right?"

That day, I learned yet another one of the most valuable life lessons on stewardship that has influenced my shopping decisions throughout my life. Because I was tuned in to the value of sales and acutely aware of my meager budget, it never occurred to me that if the item(s) were on sale now, they would go on sale again. And that was despite the fact that I would have seen those sales come around before. The seller always built things up to lure you into shopping immediately, making you think that they were doing you the favor of your lifetime.

What God has done over these years as it relates to sales is to help me see that one of the life lessons in Daddy's wisdom was far more about trusting God as a Provider than it was about how to spend my money. I'm not sure Daddy knew that, but he was definitely an instrument of laying the foundation of a significant godly principle for me. To need to stock up on something that I don't yet need, anticipating the need, can be a sure sign of not knowing how to trust God as a Provider.

The other lesson was that making impulsive, knee-jerk decisions is not wise or profitable in the long run and can sometimes be more costly than what you thought you were saving. How many times have you caught that great sale only to get home and have second thoughts about the purchase, or worse yet, have total regret about the purchase? And God forbid it was a final sale or a no refund or exchange policy

attached to the ordeal that makes that sale no longer a good thing for you after all. That lesson taught me to slow down and evaluate whether I was getting a true deal or whether I was being caught up in the "romance" of it all.

Now, to add a disclaimer note to all that you have read in this section, let me say that shopping on sale can definitely be a great stewardship action, but the caveat is to make sure that it is not an impulsive, frivolous, self-gratifying, or fear- based action. Make sure that you can afford it and that it is not an act of pride, greed, or just poor decision-making.

DON'T BORROW MONEY UNLESS IT CAN MAKE YOU MONEY

"Take no usury or interest from him, but fear your God that your brother may live with you. 37 You shall not lend him your money for usury nor lend him your food at a profit."

Leviticus 25:36-37

During those early years of marriage, we lived on a meager budget. Oftentimes, when you live on a meager budget, you are seemingly more aware of what you don't have, what you can't afford to do, and how things would be better if you just had more money. It is also often during those times that you are more tempted to borrow money or buy things on credit.

As teenagers, our parents would allow my sister and me to go shopping without them, let us choose the clothes or shoes we liked, and have the items charged to their account at the local department store. My sister was always the conservative one, thinking like a parent, showing off her maturity, and choosing things that she thought they would readily approve of. I, on the other hand, would choose something that I liked simply because I liked it, and extravagance was nowhere on my radar. On this particular shopping day, we were to buy "dress shoes." I can remember those red reptile-like shoes with the red strap up the back of the open high heels even now. And extravagant me even added a matching purse to finish the look. In my sister's eyes, it was not within a reasonable budget, and she tried to convince me to choose something less costly. I would not change my mind.

Once we were home, we showed off our loot, and my mother protested greatly about the expensive choices I had made. My sister sat back with that smug "I told you so look," knowing that she had been right. Later, in what was a private parental conversation, my sister and I were positioned where we could overhear the discussion. My mother was firm about my needing to return that matching set and choose something else, but my dad disagreed and said, "We never really gave them a budget, so we can't say that they went over one." My mother disappointedly voiced that she thought we had good sense about these things and would know better. He explained that my sister and I were two very different people and couldn't be expected to make the same kinds of decisions from the same information.

Much to my mother's dismay and my delight, his argument won out, and I got to keep those sharp red shoes and matching purse.

As I became an adult, married and on a much smaller budget than I had ever realized while living under my parents' roof, my taste for the more extravagant things of life seemed to course correct, but somehow, I believe that my dad remembered that teenager who simply picked what she liked because she liked it. One day, as he would often drop by to check on us, he struck up a conversation about money and debt. He advised me that I probably should never get a credit card because it would be too easy for me to just go buy stuff, not seeing the end of the "due date" concept. He then went on to talk about simple interest vs compound interest and why compound interest was bad. He explained that simple interest would only be the amount of interest you agree to pay to a lender for the use of their money, and once the agreed amount is set, you pay the bill in monthly installments for a set number of months until there is no balance. There is never any increase in the total amount due while the installment payments are being made. He furthered the "lesson" by saying that compound interest is when you agree to pay a set amount of interest to the lender for the use of their money, but each month that there is a balance on the debt, the lender gets to charge you interest on that balance yes, each month. So, if you borrow

$100 and the interest is 5%, your debt is $105. If you agree to pay a monthly amount of $20, you cannot control when the final debt will be paid off. If you only pay a monthly amount of $20 the first month, on the second month, and every month following, the lender gets to add that 5% to whatever the new balance is. He said then you would be paying interest on the interest. He said that was borrowing money that couldn't make you any money; as a matter of fact, compound interest would take your money.

Now, what you may not know about me is that I am wired, as I self-describe as a logical, analytical type. If it doesn't make sense to my logic, I am likely to abandon, discard, or discredit things unless I can hear a compelling argument to persuade me. I remember thinking through my dad's "lesson" that day and deciding that I didn't like interest because it meant paying someone else just to use their money. I reasoned, though, that if I ever had to use someone else's money, it would certainly only be on a simple interest basis. Compound interest was totally out of the question. Nope. I wasn't going to just give away my money. I wasn't about to make someone else rich off of me. As a result of that visit that day long ago, my perspective on borrowing was totally altered. It was another 20 years later, when my second son was in college before I got my first credit card. I had lived all of my adult life either paying as I went or putting things on layaway. It wasn't until I learned that my credit history was non-existent but necessary in modern culture that I began my credit card history. That lifestyle has led to me having an excellent credit score and a deep respect for how to handle money wisely. I am ever so grateful for such a valuable lesson.

As another one of my disclaimers, however, I would like to add that there may come a time when anyone will need to borrow money. I only hope that as that point comes in your life, these simple lessons from my dad will help you borrow money responsibly and wisely, recognizing that your best advantage is to know when your last payment will become due.

NEVER BRING YOUR CAR
HOME EMPTY

"For which of you, intending to build a tower, sitteth not down first and counteth the cost, whether he have sufficient to finish it?"

Luke 14:28

Have you ever had those moments when you got what seemed like some hokey advice, so you chuckled and tucked it away in the unnamed file folder? Well, this saying ranks high up in that category in my life. Let me explain why this one sounded so silly when I was growing up. It's like one of those things your parents say when they are trying to make a point, but the meaning of the point escapes you. The back story is that my parents owned a gas (filling) station and restaurant from the time I was five years old until I married and left home. We sold Texaco gas and had lots of customers. Because we were somewhat of a family/neighborhood business, it was not uncommon for people to come to our "store" at odd hours, often after the business was closed for the night. People would not hesitate to wake us up to pump gas when they were empty and needed to respond to their self-made emergency of poor planning. Over the years, this became a much too regular occurrence because my parents had a well-known huge compassionate streak and would always respond affirmatively.

Though we always accommodated the desperate customers, it was not a practice that my dad appreciated very much, which prompted a lecture or "teaching moment" coming our way. Once he began the lesson, whenever or whatever it might be, you knew instinctively that some great nugget was coming forth. Consequently, this one was birthed out of the continuous demands on our after-hours private life and my obvious failure to grasp its importance.

As best I could tell from observation (not necessarily by instruction), the obvious rule of thumb seemed to be if the car gasoline gauge showed below ¼ tank, fill up the car. Now, to a teenager who lived at a gas station, this example seemed just a little bit silly. Why on earth would you not put gas in the car before you run out when pumping gas seemed as easy and accessible as breathing? In my mind, again, based on observation, this seemed logical, so I surely had that particular concept down pat. That was one that didn't require any specific instruction because, of course, I would keep gas in the car, and if I didn't, I'd just pump some!

As you might have guessed by now, my overly confident alter-ego led me down an unfortunate path. In one of those arrogant days, I messed around and failed to follow the rule of common sense. And let me add that it really was not my fault. It was all totally circumstantial in that the gas that was in the car was quite adequate for me to go where I was supposed to go but remember, I was a teenager. I happened to go to a friend's house that was much further away than my original destination, and because our parents were very liberal when it came to trusting us to use good judgment, I did not see the need to ask permission. Since I had the car anyway, and there were no cell phones back in those days, it seemed like a natural progression to make just one more stop. And I almost made it, but wouldn't you know I ran out of gas almost at home.

Daddy came and rescued me with the gas can because I stopped one of the familiar travelers who came upon me in my predicament and sent him for help. You can just imagine that I was not looking forward to being rescued for this particular circumstance. I knew a lecture/lesson was guaranteed to be on the horizon. And I was not mistaken in my estimate. Since it already seemed as though Daddy lived for the "teachable moments" of life, it was as though he had been waiting for this day to come. What you have to know is that he would prolong the

lesson with all the reasons why you were getting this important nugget, and sometimes prolonging was an understatement. This particular lesson included things like "You may have an emergency and have to go to the hospital in the middle of the night." Or "Someone else might have an emergency that demanded your immediate response." Or "You might be late for work or something and make yourself late by having to stop and pump gas."

Though I was thinking things like, "What in the world does all this have to do with just putting that gas in the tank?" I was way too smart to interrupt him and way too scared to lose my driving privileges to offer any lame excuse. The important thing to note here is that, in retrospect, the lesson was so full of wisdom that I marvel even today at its relevance.

As bright and intelligent as I may appear to be based on some previous seemingly sound and wise acts of good judgment, I have to be the one in confession right now. Life has clearly proven over the years that periodically, I obviously missed the importance of the lesson and regretfully had to experience life as an adult. The confession would have to include those days when I would be very annoyed or angry with myself on the few occasions that I found myself in a hurry, jumping in the car, and then regretfully remembering that I had chosen not to stop and buy gas on the way home. The phrase from The Wizard Of Oz, "You're not in Kansas anymore," became my unspoken theme every time I was reminded that pulling up to that old Texaco pump and filling up the car with gas was a luxury that I no longer had. It took a few inconveniences and, thankfully, only one or two emergencies for me to seal that nugget deep in my mind and prevent the agony of needing to buy gas out of untimely necessity as opposed to basic wise planning. It really does pay off to "count the cost," as the scripture says, before you set out on any undertaking.

BUY A FULL TANK OF GAS; IT'S CHEAPER; DON'T SQUEEZE THE GAS PUMP; OVERFLOW EVAPORATES

"And he said also unto his disciples, there was a certain rich man, which had a steward; and the same was accused unto him that he had wasted his goods."

Luke 16:1

Note: These two sayings are being presented together because they are so closely connected, and they came together as somewhat of a continuation.

Living in a home that was attached to a gas station came with as many advantages as disadvantages. The disadvantages are not explicitly covered in this particular book because, for me, the advantages far outweighed the disadvantages. In this chapter, I am highlighting the fact that the advantages of wise counsel and sound instruction learned about cars could only have come from being raised in a home that was attached to a gas station. And this particular lesson, I am happy to report, did not come from one of my many days of poor judgment or immature behavior.

Because Daddy was known for his logical approach to problem-solving, I am convinced that much of the time, the things that he shared he learned from experience. Without being an avid reader, how could he possibly have known some of the things he shared? At any rate, this chapter will be brief but helpful.

On one of the many occasions that I was pumping gas, Daddy just happened to be in the vicinity and decided to take advantage of yet another "teaching moment." He began the conversation by asking me if I was filling the gas tank with gas. I played along with him because, in my mind, he surely knew that I was filling up the tank. So, of course, out of respect and a little bit of unspoken offense, I responded appropriately with an affirmative. That gave him the open door to give me a little tip. Once I said yes, he went on to say that filling the tank was always a good idea. His theory was that filling the tank actually saves gas, thus saving you money. He shared that a car with a full tank of gas gets better gas mileage, so you go further and have to fill up less often. He said that if you only put in a gallon or two because gas evaporates slightly in the heat of the tank, it evaporates more quickly; thus, the lesser amount of gas costs you more.

I have since then surmised that because he was on an "evaporation" roll, the following comments were inspired. He went on to add that it also made no sense to squeeze the pump handle once the cut-off valve stopped the automatic gas flow. Again, his logic was that gas evaporates, and the gas at the mouth of the tank, beyond the cut-off indicator, would evaporate way before it ever got far enough down into the tank to fuel the engine. He was adamant that it was a waste of money on both counts: to buy a lesser amount of gas or to squeeze the nozzle past the cut-off.

Now for the disclaimer here: I admit that I have never done any scientific research on my dad's theory. What I can say, though, is that over my lifetime, whether it's just been my imagination or it's been a truth, it seems to me that he was right. For all of you scientists or possible skeptics reading this, once you do your own research, please don't burst my bubble. Please let me continue to believe that this is yet another way that I am demonstrating good stewardship over the resources I have been given.

IF YOU CAN PAY YOUR
WAY YOU CAN GO

Then Nathan said to the king, "Go, do all that *is* in your heart, for the Lord *is* with you."

II Samuel 7:3

This particular saying may have been one of the most impactful sayings in my life (And forgive me because I know I have already said that several times). The principle of it influenced my sister and me to reach for anything we could imagine, but with the caveat that reaching for a dream and reaching a dream are not the same things. Actually, reaching a dream requires work, ingenuity, tenacity, and a whole lot of courage.

I was approaching my twelfth birthday, and my sister had already had her fourteenth birthday two months earlier. The World's Fair was in New York that year, and I had seen pictures of the Hemisphere, one of the main attractions of the Fair. I decided, quite precociously, I might add, that I wanted to go to the World's Fair for my birthday. After a conference with my sister, we decided that it was a great idea and that we should approach our dad with the request. We somewhat sheepishly made our approach, blurting out that we wanted to go to New York to the World's Fair for my 12th birthday. He gave it a little bit of thought and came up with what I believe (now from a parent's perspective) he thought was a foolproof response to put our request to rest. He responded, "If you can pay your own way, you can go." Now, surely he knew that he had raised two very intelligent girls in that we were already responsible for much of the business aspects of the family business. We basically ran "The Store" without much adult supervision on a regular basis, even to the extent of conducting the transactions with the vendors. We both had power of attorney to sign checks to pay for the vendors' products when our parents were away from home at very young ages.

When we got that response, our brains went into 3rd gear, and we developed a plan. My sister, the investigator, researched the cost. The Trailways Bus was the regular mode of travel for most people in our area, so she discovered first of all those children under the age of 12 only paid half the adult fare. With that in mind, and because we had been taught strong ethics, we decided that we had to travel just shy of my birthday so that we would not be doing anything unethical. The one-way adult fare from Richmond, VA, to New York City was $8.50. Thus, the child's fare was $4.25. We needed $13 to purchase tickets. Neither of us had any real means of income because getting an allowance in those days, as far as we knew, was an unknown practice.

My sister, the thinker, came up with the plan. We convinced one of our parents' farmer friends to allow us to work in his peanut fields, chopping the weeds out of the peanut vines. Though, we had never done any such thing before, our dad agreed to the plan. Our motivation was that the pay for each of us was $5 per day, so the fact that we had no clue what we were doing was irrelevant. We were smart, and we were motivated, so surely that was enough for us to do a good job. Fortunately, this was so long ago that I can now confess that we probably cut deeply into that poor farmer's profit by chopping up peanut vines along with the weeds. We worked a full week and then got ambitious and signed on with another farmer. Our plan ended with a purse so big we were ready for anything.

The moment of truth arrived, and we approached our dad with our money and reminded him of his promise that we could go if we could pay our own way. Daddy was such an amazing person in my eyes because, thinking back on the situation, I can't imagine keeping my word to such an outlandish request. Instead of backtracking, however, our parents actually went ahead with the agreement.

Even though the Trailways Bus made a stop at our "Store," our parents decided that we should catch the bus out of Richmond, VA, because there would be an "express" straight through to Grand Central Station in New York with no need for a transfer. There would be one stop along the way but no transfer. Our parents drove us to Richmond, and after giving us specific safety instructions, checking our luggage, checking our packed food, and hugging us tightly, we were on our way.

We arrived in New York without any incidents, and as we got off the bus, we found ourselves in the middle of Grand Central Station. Our mother's sister, who lived in Brooklyn, was to retrieve us from the Station. She was not readily present as we got off the bus and looked all around, and once again, the thinker said, "Moving objects don't connect; let's just stand here in the middle of the floor and wait." Surely enough, our aunt found us and scooped us up. She was far more frantic than we were. We were quite confident that all was well, just as if we had traveled alone to a major city regularly.

Our parents drove to New York later in the week, and I celebrated my 12th birthday in New York. Our aunt took us to many wonderful places, and I got to see the Hemisphere at the World's Fair. Our parents drove us back home.

I'm going to end the story here because I believe I have captured the essence of the point that this saying has shown. I began by suggesting that this one lesson has likely impacted my life in a major way, and I still believe that to be true. I can say that my life has been an ongoing adventure, taking me to the mission fields of Haiti, not knowing where I would be staying, to the mission fields of Kazakhstan, not knowing what I would be doing, and to the mission fields of Uganda not knowing how the trips would be financed. I have learned to trust in God to step out into situations that seem impossible or at the least seem unlikely, knowing that my Heavenly Father is far more faithful than even my earthly Father. God has prepared me, through that experience, to cast off obvious limitations and to expect the unexpected as long as the desires of my heart line up with His purposes and plans for my life.

DON'T ASK ME MY BUSINESS; TELL ME WHAT YOU WANT

And when he raised his eyes, he saw the traveler in the open square of the city, and the old man said, "Where are you going, and where do you come from?"

Judges 19:17

One of the great lessons I learned from my dad speaks loudly about one's integrity and one's motive. This particular saying falls in that category, and I learned its value very early in life. As I thought about how to share this saying, I thought that this time, I would begin with a question.

Have you ever (or perhaps how many times) wanted to get something from someone else, and rather than be direct and honest, simply asking for what you want or need, you beat around the bush? You may have begun with flattery, or you might have begun with laying a guilt foundation. Or you might even have stooped to drama or hysteria. In any case, your ultimate goal was to get the other person to give you what you wanted, but the mischievousness (or lack of integrity) of your own heart tainted your motives. If that has ever been your situation, then as harshly as this may sound, you were being sneaky and dishonest and really needed to check out the motive in your heart. Now, in all fairness, the approach may have been born out of the fear of rejection or the sincerity of good intentions, but the fear or the sincerity led you into a place of manipulation, whether intentional or not.

I firmly believe that my dad had lived through enough and had had enough dealings with people that he had a pretty good handle on human nature. I also believe that to the best of his ability, he wanted to teach me the importance of honesty and integrity and the dangers of misrepresenting yourself and using deceit as a method of getting what you want.

It was not uncommon for me to ask my dad for spending money or ask him to take me somewhere, or as I became a driver, to ask if I could use the car. As I was learning how to navigate through life and how to get the advantage I was seeking at the time, I developed little strategies that I thought would get me the result I wanted. It didn't take me long to realize that any approach other than an honest, direct, and respectful one was not the way to get results from my dad.

As I recall those early days when I wanted something, I can remember being a little intimidated and fearful of rejection, though I'm not sure where that came from, as my dad was very approachable and consistently generous with me.

Somehow, though, I found myself thinking that I needed skills to justify the need for my request, whatever the request might be, thus a need to calculate my approach. On this particular day, I had asked Daddy for some money, and though I cannot remember the amount now, I know that it had to be $20 or less. I would not have needed much more than that during my growing-up years. So, I sheepishly approached my dad, all poised and calculated, and I posed my question. I said, "Daddy, do you have $20?" (Again, I am just using this amount for the sake of discussion.) Once my question was out in the atmosphere, I was able to exhale. I knew I was getting ready to go in for the kill because, as I said previously, Daddy was a generous giver. News Flash!! Instead of what I expected, I got the unexpected surprise of my life. Daddy's reply was short and with no "Daddy niceness" to it. He simply said, "Don't ask me my business; just tell me what you want." I was floored. What kind of a response was that? How could I proceed with my well-thought-out cunning plan with that kind of response? Clearly, I had to regroup.

Then, as usual, there came the "teaching moment". Daddy proceeded to explain to me that how much money he had was really none of my business. He said it was a cheap, cowardly approach to asking for something. He said he did not need me to account for his money and that I needed to learn how to approach people honestly. And even though he did not use the actual word integrity, I learned a valuable lesson that day about what it meant, or perhaps I should rephrase that to "I began to learn what integrity meant" without knowing what I was learning. You can see what I mean by "began to learn" because, unfortunately, I have another similar memory that occurred one day much later when I wanted to use the car. I, thinking I was being considerate, asked, "Daddy, do you need the car today?" You could almost hear the imaginary brakes skid to a stop with a shrilling scrape. That seemingly logical, innocent question got the same response from days gone by. I couldn't believe it. Daddy was consistent, but clearly, I had not yet gotten the message. (Full disclosure, though, is that I did get better.)

We have become masterful at trying to get what we want with cunning ways and cowardly hearts, and I don't think we even have to be taught how to be that way. Out of our own insecurities and basic fear of rejection, we have learned to sweeten the pot with what I call "the okee-doke," believing it to be to our advantage. As harsh as it may sound, the truth of the matter is that it is a subtle way of dulling our sense of integrity and opening us up for more deceitful and perhaps even more treacherous habits later in life.

Now, just for the record, though it might seem otherwise, I am happy to say that in each of my untrained attempts to get something from my dad, he always came through with what I ultimately asked for, but he did indeed hold me, hostage, until I asked directly. What those experiences did for me back then has shaped me into a person of integrity who has long outlived my dad. Thankfully, I have been able to pass along to my children (and pretty much anybody else who "sets themselves up") the principle that being honest, direct, and respectful is always the triumphant way to travel.

PS Here is a coaching tip on how to make your approach when presenting your needs.

Direct: "May I have (or borrow, if appropriate) $20?"

Never say, "Do you have $20 you can spare?"

Direct: "May I use the car?"

Never "Do you know what time you'll be back with the car?"

Direct: "Can you give me a ride?"

Never "Would it be going out of your way to give me a ride?"

SHOOT THE DOG OR EVACUATE THE CITY***

"Them that sin rebuke before all, that others also may fear."

I Timothy 5:20

Note: This saying is the one saying that has traveled the world and still seems to have the same impact on the listener each time I tell it that it had on me more than 40 years ago. This is the story that I referenced in the introduction that I shared in Rwanda.

I was a well-trained but relatively young administrator in my early 30s, and I had been awarded the awesome responsibility of co-writing and implementing an inner-city substance abuse treatment program for youth. I received my social work master's degree in the field concentration of substance abuse and had several years of experience managing residential facilities for pre-adjudicated youth, both male and female. At the time of this particular appointment, I was supervising a multifaceted substance abuse treatment program. When I was selected for the position of program director, I was elated and terrified at the same time.

My duties began with securing a location and hiring a staff. A location was identified and conditionally approved in the city with easy access for the prospective staff and residents. To begin my challenges, it was discovered that one vital step had been omitted in securing the facility, and the local civic organization ultimately denied us access. Because of the underlying political implications of the program that had been commissioned by the local mayor, not opening the program was not an option, so after weeks of dead- ends, our program was relocated to an obscure site away from the city and on the grounds of the government-run minimum security facility for youth. During the securing of the facility, staffing had begun. As in many start-up government programs, unfortunately, many of the prospective employees were to be selected from a pool of somewhat "guaranteed" prospect positions. Thus, as this program was a product of the mayor upholding his promise to the citizens, some of my "hiring autonomy" was taken away. Though I had to secure qualified personnel, there was an unspoken expectation that some portion of the staff would be recovering addicts, staff who would bring the needed element of relevant experience to the treatment encounter.

Once the staff was in place and we began to service the youth, it was not very long before challenges began. One of the staff had been in recovery for a long time and, being ten years plus my senior, began to undermine my authority. He mostly tried to highlight my youth and my lack of direct experience as a drug user. He bullied the staff and the clients. He moved about with authority and arrogance. He changed the schedule without permission. He interacted with the officials at the site where we were located, giving the impression that he was the person in charge. He attempted to screen the prospective clients. He basically made my life miserable. The situation became so serious that the staff began coming to me, appealing to me, then pleading with me to do something. I knew that as a supervisor, I was losing their respect and their trust.

Unfortunately, I had allowed the man to intimidate me so tremendously, shaking all my confidence, that I was actually afraid to challenge him. I tried manipulating him, but he was far more masterful at that game. I tried reasoning with him, but he simply dismissed my suggestions. It seemed as though he was taking over the program. The good news is that intimidation and fear will only reside in me for a season before my integrity rises up and pushes me out into the ring to fight. Being pushed out to fight but not knowing how to even throw the first punch, I did the one thing I knew to do: I called my dad long distance.

As I was lamenting on the phone, begging my dad to help me with what to do, he did what only my dad could do.

Instead of offering me any consolation or advice, he asked me a simple question in a complex form, meaning it was kind of a two-in-one question. That question has influenced my life as a supervisor/administrator and helped me to navigate through many tough situations over the years.

Daddy asked the question, "If you had a dog with rabies and a city full of people, which would you do? Would you shoot the dog or evacuate the city?" That was it. He made no further comment and left me to figure things out on my own.

After I got off the phone, I sat there at my desk for what seemed like an eternity before the essence of that question sunk in. I sat there, realizing how foolish one of the answers would be. I then seemed to have an encounter with some strength that I didn't remember I had, and I heard a plan of determination begin to develop.

It was already quite late in the workday, and of course, that staff person was long gone for the day. I went home that evening a little scared but a whole lot more determined.

The next morning, when he arrived at his chosen hour, I invited him into my office. While sitting authoritatively behind my desk, I asked him to have a seat. Once he was seated, I handed him his dismissal letter, announced that he was fired, and instructed him to please get up, gather his belongings, and leave the premises immediately. I had security on standby, poised and ready in the event I needed backup. I needed no backup. That man was so stunned that he didn't even respond. He stood up, looking at me in disbelief, and because I was sitting and didn't want him towering over me, I stood up with confidence. Without a word, he abruptly turned and walked out. I had given no warning to the staff, but they knew that something serious was going on, possibly just from my demeanor. They never confessed to it, but I suspect they were lurking outside my office door, trying to hear what was happening and, in all fairness to them, trying to make sure I was all right. Once the staff saw him brush past them and go to his desk to gather his things, everyone was almost motionless. They were definitely speechless. Once I officially made them aware of what had happened, they started applauding me and rejoicing shamelessly. They had no idea the sigh of relief I had exhaled as I saw that figure leave my office without protest.

That powerful lesson that was born out of a simple two-part question could have given me the idea to rename this story "How To Handle A Bully, Especially A 'Public' Bully," so if you ever want to reuse this one, you have my permission to title it your way. This lesson has been a North Star throughout my life and my career, and my hope is that it is a lesson that will live on in the lives of others when they encounter a similar situation.

IF THE DOG BITES YOU THE FIRST TIME

"As a dog returneth to his vomit, so a fool returneth to his folly."

Proverbs 26:11

This chapter may be one of the shortest ones partly because the saying is pretty simple, but the saying itself is one of the longest sayings. The full saying is, "If the dog bites you the first time, it's the dog's fault, but if he bites you the second time, it's your fault.

Possibly unlike most of you, there were many days growing up when I would make a decision that was clearly unwise and detrimental to my well-being. To add insult to injury, I would then make the same or similar decision more than once.

On one such occasion, my older brother and I were playing outside in the coldest of winter. There had been snow and ice on the rooftops that had begun to melt. The roof was a slanted tin roof, and as the weather warmed and the thaw started, the most beautiful icicles would form. We would play under the icicles and throw rocks at the longer ones to see if we could knock them off the roof. My brother had successfully managed to hit a few and had encouraged me to try. Being much shorter, I had to stand much closer. I had made myself very vulnerable by trusting my brother because he had made things look so easy, so I would throw my rock and run to prevent the ice from falling on my head. At one point, I was much too close to the roof and not nearly fast enough in my running, and ice fell on my head. It was fun and funny, and though my head was wet from the falling ice, I repeated my actions a few times, getting my head wetter and wetter. Finally, I made the grand gesture and knocked off an icicle, and when it came, so did an entire sheet of ice from the roof. I got trapped under a pointed piece of melting ice that made a cut in the top of my head that required some adult intervention. Once the excitement was over and sufficient threats had been made to my brother, my dad was seeking an explanation. In my childlike innocence, I offered some information that gifted me with this quote. I simply let Daddy know that I had knocked off a lot of the ice, and when it fell on my head, it only hurt a little but mostly just made my hair wet. He listened somewhat impatiently, which gave me a clue that my information was not going to be to my advantage. He asked, "So you had already been hit in the head?" I shook my head in the affirmative. He said, "And it hurt your head when the ice hit it?" I shook my head in the affirmative again. He was so serious as he responded. He simply said, "If the dog bites you the first time, it's the dog's fault, but if he bites you the second time, it's your fault.

You can probably figure out by now that that decision was a big mistake on my part, but unfortunately, I put too much trust in my brother, and I had a few more scrapes in life before I caught on.

Another incident arose when I let my brother convince me that it was perfectly safe to use a large metal sign shaped like a Coca-Cola bottle cap as a sled to glide down an embankment near our house. It had been a display sign that had been destroyed somehow (I can't remember the details) and was lying on the ground. When torn apart, both sides were shaped like a wide metal bowl. The unfortunate part is that the metal edges were much too sharp to be used as a toy. My brother made his slide down the hill seem so effortless, so I was eager to try it, too. I did indeed try only to have the "bowl" overturn and cause my knees and elbows to be sufficiently scraped. I didn't need Daddy to tell me this time that trusting my brother in outside play was not profitable for me and that I was never trusting him with one of his schemes again. Tragically, where my brother was concerned, it took quite a few scrapes and bruises before I realized the principle, "If the dog bites you the first time, it's the dog's fault. If he bites you the second time, it's your fault. The good news is that, finally, it became a lesson well learned!

I TAUGHT YOU RIGHT
FROM WRONG

"Wherefore, my beloved, as ye have always obeyed, not as in my presence only, but now much more in my absence, work out your own salvation with fear and trembling."

Philippians 2:12

Imagine being sixteen years old and preparing for your first real date. You know, the one where the boy comes to your house to pick you up in the family car and drives you away. Well, that's the situation that prompted this particular saying.

We lived in a public place on a main highway in rural Virginia, and our private living quarters were attached to the business. We called it "The Store" when, in actuality, it was a barbecue restaurant, gas station, and hangout spot with a pool table and a jukebox. There was always somebody coming and going, and the weekends were like prime time. Many of our friends and schoolmates gathered there, as well as even more adults. Parents even brought their children along as part of the weekly family outing.

Even though we saw boys all the time, and there was certainly an ample amount of flirting and bantering back and forth, no part of those interactions was considered dating.

Our parents had already established what I believe could be called "dating rules," so my sister and I had no illusions about when we would be able to have our first "official date." Dating was permitted only after you became sixteen years old. Since my sister was two years older, she had already broken the ice, so my turn came pretty easily. But to make sure there was no misunderstanding on my part, as was my nature, I asked a few questions. Not that I can be sure now, but many of my questions may have been prompted by the observations I had made from many of our friends. We had friends that had a clear and definite curfew established by their fathers and pretty much set in cement. Yet regularly, we watched some of them literally sit at our store and watch the clock to guarantee that they would not make curfew. Those friends also were likely to venture off into some places that were known to be off-limits and were also likely to make some decisions that, if known, would have surely gotten them grounded.

With all this knowledge before me, for my first date, I decided to ask my dad a curfew question. I remember clearly asking Daddy what time I had to be home. His response was yet another one of those that, depending on the kid, could certainly lead to some unhealthy results.

Knowing your children became a crucial parenting skill that I would fully learn to appreciate as a parent. When I posed my question, Daddy simply responded, "You know right from wrong. I taught you right from wrong". That was it! He then moved on with whatever he had been doing and didn't even look back.

As I reflect on that incident even today, I am engulfed with a sense of amusement and humility simultaneously. The amusing thought was, "Wow! Daddy must have been a brave soldier to give us that kind of freedom", but instantly, the serious level of trust he had in us began to move me to a place of total humility. His confidence is lodged in our integrity. He trusted the integrity and the wisdom he had imparted to us. The amazing thing about all of this and the proof that as a parent, you can indeed instill a strong measure of integrity in your children can be found in the fact that my sister and I, though we never had a curfew, came home earlier than most kids that we knew. We would even make fun of our friends who had curfews but seemingly intentionally failed to meet them.

The decisions that we made during those teenage years afforded us so many valuable life opportunities. I am reminded of the scripture that says, "You are faithful over a few things; I will make you ruler over many." As we grew, there was very little that was withheld from us based on the trust that had been established between us and our dad.

Even at a very young age, we both had power of attorney to sign our parents' signatures on bank checks to pay the vendors during parental absence. Granted, that was mostly because we had been signing checks without bank authorization, so our parents were called in, and it was suggested that they make things official. I was barely 12 years old back then, yet we were trusted with such adult responsibility. In our later years, we were able to drive the car unrestrained and handle business affairs and family affairs with no cause for our parents to be concerned. So, as I consider the slightly unorthodox (which is arguable) yet effective style in which we were parented, I am so grateful for the lessons learned that have shaped our character over the years, and today, both of us are finding ourselves in places of authority and responsibility.

COMMON SENSE AIN'T
THAT COMMON

"All things are lawful for me, but not all things are helpful; all things are lawful for me, but not all things edify."

I Corinthians 6:12

I believe that I shared earlier that I am somewhat of a "logical/ analytical," so I am regularly weighing the situation and making a determination whether it is profitable for me (or anyone else) to continue on the present course, whatever that course may be. It is that strong characteristic that often prompted this saying being introduced in this chapter.

In my early years, I was often in an environment where I would observe others making what I considered really dumb decisions. At our place of business, I encountered many adults who would say and do things that would surely lead to some kind of conflict. At school I would see my peers make decisions that would surely get them in trouble. And even at church, which I loved, I would see or maybe even be involved in some act of foolishness that did not end well for those of us who participated. It was on one of these many occasions that I got to hear this current saying, realizing that the times I heard it over the years are too numerous to try to remember, so I will only include a few. This particular account involved my maternal uncle and one of his many escapades. He had a reputation for being a fighter, and fighting the police was not out of the ordinary for him. I was quite young at the time and was listening to what was called "Grown people's conversation" as I heard what seemed like the most senseless conversation unfold. Allegedly, my uncle had once again gotten into a slight altercation with the local police and had been arrested.

Since this was clearly not the first time this had happened, and allegedly, he had been warned that it better not happen again, there was no logical reason in my mind that he would ever have engaged in such an act. As the conversation continued, in my child's mind, I was totally baffled, and unfortunately, my thoughts came out of my mouth in the midst of that "grown people's conversation." I whispered somewhat too loudly, "That didn't make good sense. Common sense should tell you that you are not supposed to fight with the police." Instead of scolding me as I expected, my dad turned around and said, "Common sense ain't that common."

Incidents like that one seemed to have been prevalent throughout those years because I got to hear that sentence fairly regularly. When my older brother would do outlandish things and get in trouble, I would, out of bewilderment, utter that common sense should tell you not to do that, and Daddy would remind me that common sense ain't that common. My brother would have once again failed to fulfill his duties at the store or would go driving without permission or any number of other unwise things. It was a guarantee that when my logical question would come forth about why he would do whatever the act was because it just didn't make good sense, I got the same response," Common sense ain't that common."

In later years, as I became more invested in the thoughts and welfare of others, the issue would be things like it didn't make sense for people to run out of gas or it didn't make sense not to pay parking tickets because they double when you don't pay them or it didn't make sense to buy things they didn't need just because they were on sale, and the response was always the same. I believe in this instance; my dad was also trying to teach me a much greater lesson than the obvious. I believe he wanted me to see that constantly trying to figure out why other people do what they do and then allowing their decisions to baffle or frustrate me was not helpful (profitable) to me in that I couldn't change one thing about it. To spend that kind of time judging others is definitely not profitable, and the best solution is to pay attention to your own decisions and make sure they do indeed "make good sense. It is a challenging process for me so much of the time, and it really doesn't make good sense for me to expend that kind of energy, which means that even for me, I have yet to master the principle that "Common sense ain't that common."

CAN'T MEASURE OTHER PEOPLE WITH YOUR OWN MEASURING STICK

"Judge not, that you be not judged. 2 For with what judgment you judge you will be judged; and with the measure you use, it will be measured back to you."

Matthew 7:1-2

One of the greatest challenges I faced growing up that continues to haunt me even today is trying to understand why people do what they do, so this chapter is somewhat of a continuation of the previous one. Most of the time, when this saying was spoken, it would be associated with some complaint I was making about an injustice that I had either experienced or witnessed. And I find myself using the phrase on myself in my embarrassingly numerous self-talk conversations.

By now, one would think that my life experiences with my fellow humans should have taught me that some people are not always who they appear to be, that they don't always have your best interest at heart, that their own insecurities and emotional wounds can emanate hurt; and that they simply cannot be trusted. However, I can mostly be considered an optimist when it comes to fellow humans, and I usually am willing to give "the benefit of the doubt" before I am proven wrong.

A very painful incident occurred for me several years ago when I was betrayed by a friend in the most unnecessary way. We were having a casual and totally meaningless conversation about the likely election of one of our friends to a high position. We both nodded (I thought, in innocent agreement) that he would likely get the appointment because he was so well-known and his family so well-liked. I engaged in that conversation with a pure heart and a congratulatory spirit. The conversation moved on to another meaningless casual conversation before we parted ways.

In a few days, I was privately confronted by a close family member of the candidate, loving but clearly hurt that I would say something so mean about the candidate's appointment. He was so disappointed that I would say something negative about anyone in their family because they considered me a true friend and ally. I was so floored by the encounter that I stood there speechless. Once I regrouped, I devastatingly realized who had to have spread that lie. There was only one person I had the conversation with, and even if I had been cruel enough or stupid enough to gossip about anyone else, it would certainly not have been about a friend to a friend, knowing how close we both were to the family.

I confessed to the person who confronted me that I had indeed engaged in a conversation on the matter but that nothing even close to derogatory had been said. I had simply agreed that his loved one was the most likely candidate. The truth and love of my heart clearly must have shone through because he stood there puzzled and said out loud, "I wonder why she would do such a thing. I thought she was your friend." I apologized for any confusion or hurt my involvement in the conversation may have caused, and he gave me a loving hug and assured me that he believed that I had not done anything to betray our mutual trust.

For weeks, I trod very lightly around my "friend," trying to understand why she would do such a thing. It was a very mean thing to do. It lacked integrity; it was divisive; it was sneaky; and it clearly had an ill intent. I kept thinking, "I would never do anyone like that.

That's being an ugly talebearer." Then I heard my Daddy's voice in my head reminding me that I cannot measure other people by my own measuring stick, so I chose to forgive her and to make a gesture to let her know that I knew of the betrayal.

I do confess that that one incident taught me a valuable lesson about people. We can never know what evil lurks in the hearts of others, even those we believe are our friends that we think we can trust. So, it is crystal clear that we need to make sure that whatever we say, whether casually or innocently, especially if it includes an absent party, is edifying in every way, and we'd better be prepared to righteously defend anything we say if confronted. It also taught me that everyone that you think is your friend is not your friend. Finally, it taught me that I can literally influence/dictate the direction of any conversation I am engaged in, and if I discover that I can't, I'd better get far away from it as quickly as possible.

EDUCATION IS
EXPENSIVE

"Looking carefully lest anyone fall short of the grace of God; lest any root of bitterness springing up cause trouble, and by this, many become defiled; 16 lest there be any fornicator or profane person like Esau, who for one morsel of food sold his birthright. 17 For you know that afterward, when he wanted to inherit the blessing, he was rejected, for he found no place for repentance, though he sought it diligently with tears."

Hebrews 12:15-1

As you can imagine, over the years, I have made some incredibly unwise, sometimes downright stupid decisions. If I was to elaborate on just one month of my life, I would be writing an epic novel instead of a few brief memories of my Father. This saying was one I heard often because I seemed to be a master at doing things that I would later regret. The first time I heard it, I thought my dad was talking about formal education, but it didn't take me long to figure out he was sharing an impactful life principle.

The principle is so relevant to nearly any life decision that it becomes hard to separate which situations may be more appropriately applied. I remember saying some things I didn't need to say about a person, and of course, the recipient of the conversation turned out to be the talebearer, so the action came back to bite me. Even though I knew I was wrong and that I was guilty, I had the nerve to be upset with the talebearer. It damaged two relationships. I could hear my dad's voice saying, "Education is expensive," as I thought about the cost of that well-learned lesson. The cost was high, but the lesson was well learned: never say anything that you wouldn't want repeated.

I was once looking to buy some clothes and was on a serious budget, so I went to a discount store to make my money stretch. I got what looked really nice upon purchase, but it didn't take long for my bargain to transform into a dud. The fabric stretched rather than my money, and the color faded just like my investment. Yet again, I could hear "education is expensive," as I learned that bargains don't often live up to their name.

And dare I talk about the time I was going to an unfamiliar destination, and I asked a stranger at the gas station for directions and ended up lost and late (of course, these were the days before even MapQuest, let alone GPS). The significance is that rushing, I had left my directions at home and didn't want to be late by returning to get them.

Not only was I late, but I was also frustrated and disappointed that I had let down others who were counting on me.

And I'm certainly not proud of the time I ran out of gas after breaking the cardinal rule of never bringing the car home empty and had to endure the criticism and chastisement of my rescuer. Personal decision educational costs are the worst.

In more recent years, the high cost of education has had more to do with indecision rather than wrong decisions. I do a lot of traveling, and usually, airfare is closely linked to how much lead time you have to book your travel. Way too many times, I have checked out airfare, and for some seemingly logical reason, I did not book the flight at that time. Either the cost was too high, and I would wait to see if it would come down (duh), or the flight time was inconvenient, and I wanted to be certain I wanted to accept what was offered, or maybe even I just wanted to mull it over a bit more. Regardless of my logic, it nearly always ended up costing me more than the original price.

Parenting has afforded me the opportunity to share this saying maybe even more than any others. As I have watched my children make some of the most asinine decisions (of course, that's only from my viewpoint) that have guaranteed unfavorable outcomes, I have reminded them of the cost of the decision that got them that particular result. The amusing (and maybe even ironic) part about my input is that I heard it so much growing up that you would think more compassion would flow from my lips. The truth of the matter is that the fact that education is expensive will likely live on in history as one of the profound truths of our time.

IF THEY TALKING ABOUT YOU, IT'S BECAUSE YOU HAVE SOMETHING THEY WANT

"Moreover, you see and hear that not only at Ephesus but throughout almost all of Asia, Paul has persuaded and turned away many people, saying that they are not gods who are made with hands."

Acts 19:26

Though I believe it was probably my father's way of making me feel better about myself, this saying was likely my first lesson on the cruelty of envy and jealousy. Very early in life, I always knew that I looked different than my other immediate family members, distant cousins, or even my friends. I wasn't sure what the problem was until I started getting nicknames and negative references to my eye color. That was how I figured out the problem. At the time, I was one of five siblings and likely number four of about 12 grandchildren, and I was the only person around with gray eyes. In the Black community in the early 50s and 60s, especially in the rural south, that was somewhat of an anomaly.

My paternal grandmother was a very fair-skinned, short little lady with long hair and blue eyes, but that meant very little to me because, to me, she was just Grandma. All of my family members that I encountered on a regular basis had beautiful brown eyes, with maybe the exception of my one elderly uncle, and I wasn't sophisticated enough to equate his eye color to my own. It is likely that having gray eyes would have been no big deal in my world if so many other people hadn't made it a big deal. Thus, it was a big deal.

The first time I can remember being sad about my eye color was when my older siblings started telling me I was adopted. They even said mean things like "I was the milkman's child." (Back then, milk was delivered to our house.) I got teased regularly, constantly being the source of their cruel jokes. It was an unhappy time for me because all I wanted was to be like everybody else and not be ostracized. My cousins would also join in when they came to visit, and I learned to grow more and more insecure and more and more isolated. I learned how to entertain myself, to comfort myself, and to develop the habits of an introvert. Though my personality was very friendly, I still had more contentment when I was alone. I learned to write poems, plays, and songs during those years.

There was this one occasion when there seemed to be a conspiracy formed by several youngsters, and I was the target. They were whispering about me, and when I came closer, everybody stopped talking and broke into laughter. When I asked what was so funny, one of them had the cruel courage to say, "You." That didn't make any sense to me because I had only just walked up and certainly had not done anything that warranted laughter. This time, unlike others, I was more hurt than usual, and I ran off crying. My Dad discovered me in an isolated spot crying and immediately wanted to hear what could possibly have me so upset. Through the tears, I was able to explain that the other kids were talking about me and laughing about me, and I didn't know why.

If there was ever a time that I thought my dad was the greatest Dad in the whole world, it was that day. He did not use the time to console me with words of comfort, sympathy, or pity; he decided to take another approach. He said that people are always going to say things about me that I may not like or even understand, but not to worry about it. He went on to explain that when people talk about you and try to make you feel bad about who you are, it's because you have something that they want. He didn't say anything about people being mean, cruel, envious, or jealous. He really didn't focus on them too much at all. He focused on me and gave me a survival tool that would come in handy for many years to come. What he added, however, which might have been the most valuable component of all, is that I never have to do anything to show off what I have or be unkind to them; I just have to remember that how God made me is quite good enough without ever having to prove it. I may have something that some other person wants, but I only have it because God gave it to me.

How that really translates in life-application terms is that there are characteristics, gifts, and talents that God has given me that are admired by others. The crucial component, though, is that whatever admirable characteristics I may have been given, they come with great responsibility not to be used for my aggrandizement but for His glory. My life should be lived in such a way that others want what I have, not really from "me" but rather from the God who has given them to me. And for the unfortunate few who may not understand the importance of what or possibly even "why" God has chosen to make me the way that I am, hopefully, they will catch a glimpse of their own value and live a life of gratitude so that God's gift to them can shine through.

I CAN ALWAYS GET ANOTHER CAR; I CAN NEVER GET ANOTHER YOU

"Do not lay up for yourselves treasures on earth, where moth and rust destroy and where thieves break in and steal; 20 but lay up for yourselves treasures in heaven, where neither moth nor rust destroys and where thieves do not break in and steal."

Matthew 6:19-20

You will often hear me say that this saying may have been the most influential of them all, but that is only because so much of who I am has been dictated by so many of these sayings. But honestly, this one is way up there at the top of the list. This one has guided my attitude toward material things, has dominated my parenting style, and has made me extremely generous with extending grace when seemingly suffering a loss of something deemed valuable.

This saying was introduced when I was a relatively new driver at age sixteen. My Dad was known for liking new cars. As a little girl, it seemed to me that he bought them regularly. I can remember a Chevrolet, then a Ford, then another Chevrolet, then a Chevrolet again, which leads me to the incident in question.

The good thing about Daddy and his cars is that the cars were never too good for us to drive. My sister, who is two years older, had been driving Daddy's vehicles regularly before I came of age, so it was a foregone conclusion that I, too, would have easy access to the car. He liked for us to be independent, and he encouraged us to experience full life experiences.

He had bought a brand-new Chevrolet Impala with all the bells and whistles. It had power steering, power windows, a fully automatic transmission, and an eight-track tape deck. It was a chocolate brown sort of color, and it was totally sleek and cool. And it was likely the envy of many of his friends and acquaintances, which made things seemingly more notable in my mind.

It was choir rehearsal night for those of us in the "Junior Choir," and I needed to drive to church. Our house (The Store) was about 5 miles from our church, and it was routine for Daddy to allow us to drive the car pretty much anywhere we needed to go. Since my sister was now away at college, I pretty much had a free run of the car. I drove to rehearsal, and because it was an evening rehearsal, it was dark as I left the church and returned home. To compound driving safety, heavy rain had begun while we were in rehearsal and was still pouring as I started home.

When I left the side road where the church was and made my way out to the main road where our house was situated just four miles away, I cautiously pulled away from the stop sign onto the main road. In a few hundred yards from entering the highway, there was a curve bending to the right. As I entered the curve, I hit a pocket of water, hydro- planed across the ditch, and got stuck in the mud.

Fortunately, because I was driving so cautiously, I wasn't injured in any way, but just imagine the racing beat of my heart and then the overwhelming feeling of dread when it hit me, "I had wrecked my dad's brand-new car"!

It wasn't very long before a familiar face pulled up alongside the car, and seeing the situation helped me across the muddy ditch and drove us to my house. As soon as my dad heard what had happened, with help from his friends, he got the car out of the mud and drove it home. I was waiting not so bravely as I watched the muddy car pull into the yard. Daddy got out. He walked all around the car. He stood there for what seemed like an eternity, and then he came toward me. His first question was, "Are you alright?" Once I sheepishly said that I was okay, he said the most remarkable thing any child can ever hear from their parent. He said, "I can always get another car, but I can never get another you." I think he said some other words, too, but to this day, I cannot remember anything else.

That one experience was a definite "watershed moment" for me. Even though I was only a teenager, that one declaration of my value being worth more than the most valued treasure instilled an appreciation for human value and affirmation that has become a part of who I am. It has shown up more times than I can ever count as I raised children; children who were prone to break things, lose things, and mar things. Even as a more seasoned adult with adult children, grandchildren, and great-grands, I have been inwardly trained to show compassion during a time when disappointment, discipline, or chastisement might be expected after some earthly catastrophe.

I guess you can say I learned two lessons that night: human life is far more valuable than material things, and be aware of how easy it is to make material things your idol.

Idolizing treasures puts both you and them in a dangerous place.

YOU DON'T HAVE TO PAY PEOPLE TO GET ALONG WITH THEM

"Let me pass through your land; I will keep strictly to the road, and I will turn neither to the right nor to the left. 28 You shall sell me food for money, that I may eat, and give me water for money, that I may drink; only let me pass through on foot,"

Deuteronomy 2:27-28

As owners of a public business, it was seemingly understood that your customers were to always be treated graciously, even if they were not being so gracious. Daddy would say, "You don't have to pay people to get along with them," which really translated into if you are the paying customer, then you don't have to pay your money for poor service, whether it was rude, disrespectful, or incompetent. You, the paying customer, earned the right to be treated with some level of dignity and respect, and receiving a little "above and beyond service" was always a plus.

My two siblings and I worked in our parents' "store" all of our childhood years. My sister and I, particularly, though, had a surprising way of going out of our way to take good care of our regular customers. Specifically, there was a carload of neighbors that worked in the shipyard about one hour away, and after work daily, they would stop at the store on their way home. They were friends of our parents, and their children were friends of ours, either from school or church. Because they stopped so regularly and they ordered basically the same thing each day, we learned to anticipate their orders. We began preparing their orders around the time we knew they would be arriving, and as each man came in for his purchase, we would proudly present him with the one prepared just for him. It became a game for us and a treat for them. Over the years, well after the store was sold, those men would often tease us about the way we treated them during those days and would encourage and applaud us even as adults.

Those experiences, along with so many others, instilled in me a certain expectation of being treated with a level of respect and courtesy, even if not with bubbling enthusiasm. The disadvantage to such high-level expectations is that sometimes, it can cause you to become intolerant when the welcomed response as a customer goes a little sour, especially when you have already spent your money.

A significant example of this saying happened to me back in the late 90s while my middle son, who is now 47 years old at the time of this writing, was in college. It was Christmastime, and his school was in a cold winter climate, so I bought some black leather gloves as a part of his gift. On Christmas morning, when he opened his gift, we discovered that the gloves were two gloves of the same hand. Considering college Christmas break was over a span of several days, I didn't panic. I knew I had time to fix the problem. In a day or so, I simply took the gloves back to Burlington Coat Factory, where I had done the bulk of my shopping.

For those of you old enough to remember Burlington back then, they were a great place to shop for families on a budget, and they carried a wide variety of merchandise to make one-stop shopping easier. However, the company also had a no refund-exchange-only store policy, which could sometimes be very troublesome for the customers.

I arrived at the store from which I had made the purchase, approached the manager, and explained my plight. He directed me to simply go and make a replacement selection. What he was unaware of is that I had already tried to locate another pair of gloves prior to asking for a manager because as I searched, I discovered that all the gloves in the store were of the same hand, so I couldn't even open a new set and make a match. It seemed obvious to me that since the problem was so pervasive, it was clearly a manufacturing defect that all the gloves were of the same hand. Holding to company policy, the manager apologized and recommended that I try another Burlington. (This was before the days of computers on a company-wide connected network.) A bit disappointed but determined, off I went to 3 different stores within a 40-mile radius. No success. All the stores had the same problem. As the break was ending soon and my son still needed gloves, I went back to the original store and demanded a refund. The manager indignantly held his ground. I was so furious because I could not believe that I would have to suffer a loss because of an issue that I did not create. Still determined to get satisfaction, I called, then ultimately wrote to the Burlington headquarters, made my case, and asked for a refund. Nope. Company policy forbade that. It was the rule. In my indignance, I explained to the corporate representative that man had made the rule and, therefore, man could make an exception to the rule. I went on to explain that an exception should be in place for those times when the company could not stand by their product, especially when refusing to make the exception was totally unfair to the customer. Finally, because I was now out of time, I went to another department store, bought my son some gloves, went back to Burlington, and exchanged the gloves for a dress. The dress price was slightly higher than the price of the gloves, so I paid them the less-than $1.00 difference, vowing not to have even one penny of store credit left. Even today, I refuse to shop in the Burlington stores, and hopefully, that customer-unfriendly policy will have long been replaced with a policy that reflects more customer value.

DON'T EVER TELL
SOMEONE ELSE
EVERYTHING YOU KNOW

"At that time, Berodach-Baladan, the son of Baladan, king of Babylon, sent letters and a present to Hezekiah, for he heard that Hezekiah had been sick. 13 And Hezekiah was attentive to them and showed them all the house of his treasures—the silver and gold, the spices and precious ointment, and all his armory—all that was found among his treasures. There was nothing in his house or in all his dominion that Hezekiah did not show them."

II Kings 20:12-13

Sometimes, when I think about some of my Daddy's sayings, I stop and chuckle at the circumstances under which that particular one was said. This saying is one of them. Daddy knew I was a talker, and he knew that I could be somewhat of a snitch if my siblings had done something that might get us all in trouble. He knew I was never trying to go down with the ship, so I believe he was attempting to put some guardrails on me before too much talking got me into trouble. I'm not sure he was well-versed enough to know the scripture in Psalms 141:3: "Set a guard, O Lord, over my mouth; Keep watch over the door of my lips," I think he was simply operating from his amazing place of wisdom.

The way this saying was introduced to me actually came with a second and a third clause, but I thought that would make this already long title much too long. The saying actually says, "Don't ever tell someone else everything you know because then they will know what you know plus what they know; that will make them know way more than you."

The first time I heard him say this one, being the logical, analytical type that I am, it really caused me to "pause and ponder." My logic would never have brought me to such a place, and I was intrigued by the implications. Possibly, it was my sense of pride or ego that kicked in, but I knew I didn't take any pleasure in the thought of knowing that I had contributed to having other people walking around knowing way more than I did.

I am sure that when I heard this saying, Daddy was not really trying to scare me or make me become full of pride; I rather wanted to think that it was his wise way of helping me know that it is perfectly acceptable to only give the necessary details. In other words, you do not need to add information that is not being requested. I found that most true in the times when I was unable to do something that someone else was imposing on me, and my "no" always came with an explanation or defense. The scripture "Let your yes be yes and your no be no" was not anywhere in the picture back then, but it is a scripture that helps with our honesty and our integrity, usually honesty with ourselves.

It also becomes quite handy when you are asked a question or asked to verify some observed or overheard account of something. It might be couched in a warning like "Just stick to the facts." Any Perry Mason buff could tell you that. If you were not asked about your interpretation of the facts, what the other person looked like they meant, or why you think they said it that way, then keep your mouth shut because you are talking too much.

I am working on this one daily because I find that I willingly offer way too much information when responding to a question or perhaps just sharing an account of something. I am not always even conscious of how much unnecessary information the recipient has gotten until it is too late. To clarify, it is not false information, just unnecessary information, so even at this late stage in my life, I am still mastering the art of not telling everything I know. This is not because Daddy said it makes the other person know more than you, but I rather think that it is because it could lead to a situation like King Hezekiah, who showed his royal visitors much more than they needed to see, and it caused him to be robbed of everything precious in his kingdom. I believe that telling more than you need to can literally rob you of what has been designated only for you.

IT'S NEVER AN INCONVENIENCE TO BE A BLESSING

"Finally, all of you be of one mind, having compassion for one another; love as brothers, be tenderhearted, be courteous; 9 not returning evil for evil or reviling for reviling, but on the contrary, blessing, knowing that you were called to this, that you might inherit a blessing."

I Peter 3:7-9

Growing up, we had a wonderful example in our parents of what it means to help others, sometimes in their times of need and sometimes just because it was a good, thoughtful thing to do. Our house was often the refuge for family members who needed an extended stay, and it was the summer vacation spot for many of our city cousins whose parents needed to work and have their children safe during summer break.

On a seemingly smaller scale than overnight stays in our home were what we might call the days "random acts of kindness" that we would witness our Dad being the donor of. He would just drop by unannounced and have friendly visits with whoever might cross his mind (something common in tightly-knit rural communities), and

sometimes, our Dad would let us tag along on one of his visits when he was just out "seemingly" roaming around. It was on one such occasion that I was introduced to this current saying, "It's never an inconvenience to be a blessing."

There were quite a few widows and several elderly folks in our area. Daddy loved to be out and about, so he would randomly stop in on folks during his travels. This day, he stopped in on a couple who didn't seem to have any apparent need from a child's point of view, but I was happy just to be out and about with him, so a reason was unimportant to me. These nice people had a truck and a car. They had a tractor and a nice house. They were elderly (or at least I thought so), and they had no children. They lived on a farm where I am sure there was always plenty to do, so they always seemed to be working around the farm. The husband was the superintendent of our Sunday School, and it was not uncommon for him to give people rides to church. He and his wife were always really nice to us children, so I was well acquainted with them.

We stopped by their house, and we were invited inside. We were offered some refreshments but didn't accept any. After a while of casual adult conversation, Daddy was ready to go. (It was rare that he sat down on his visits.) The friendly conversation ended, and we made our way back to the car. We were in the car, and I was very curious about why we had stopped there, so I asked him about the visit. Daddy's response was puzzling in that it meant to my child translations that it was basically for no reason; he just thought he would stop and say hello. I suppose he could see the puzzled look on my face, so without any more questions from me; he commented that it's nice to just stop and show people that you care, even if it means going a little out of your way. He added that it's never an inconvenience to be a blessing. That simple phrase has stuck with me over all these years.

I'm not sure that I actually heard that expression verbalized much after that day, but it was lived before me regularly. If someone needed a ride, needed a flat repaired, or needed help while stranded on the highway, Daddy was going to do whatever it took to be of assistance. And it was not uncommon for him to send one of us to the rescue as we became older. We were basically trained to be a blessing whenever and wherever we could.

There are numerous examples of that saying playing out in our lives other than the obvious ones of lending a helping hand or paying a friendly visit. For example, I have been given the special gift of having both my maternal and paternal grandmothers live with us at different intervals in my life. My maternal grandmother was with us during many of the years we lived at the store, years of my childhood. My paternal grandmother was with my parents after I was an adult and living away from home, but I was a regular visitor there, so I got to witness the times firsthand. In both cases, though both my parents had other siblings who lived locally, our house was the acceptable alternative, revealing the heart of that saying, "It's never an inconvenience to be a blessing.

I am so grateful for the influence that attitude has had on my life and how it has contributed to my willingness to provide temporary (and sometimes long-term) shelter for non-family members as well as my own family. I am grateful for the readiness without hesitation to render aid to a person in need without motive or expectation of compensation. I am grateful that as I navigate through this life's journey, I can be guided by the saying that it is never an inconvenience to be a blessing, and my prayer is that I have demonstrated that principle among my children over their development years such that they now live by it and is teaching it to their children.

JUST BECAUSE IT LOOKS GOOD DOESN'T MEAN IT'S GOOD FOR YOU

"So, when the woman saw that the tree was good for food, that it was pleasant to the eyes, and a tree desirable to make one wise, she took of its fruit and ate. She also gave to her husband with her, and he ate."

Genesis 3:6

This saying could probably be renamed one of many familiar sayings we have likely heard over the years. Sayings like, "Everything that glitters ain't gold," or "You can't judge a book by its cover," or even "The grass always looks greener on the other side of the fence," might be among them. I am convinced that this one will fit anyone at some point in their life.

The saying brings back to my mind the times that I would make a decision about something that I was sure was the perfect decision for me, only to have it turn out to be one of the worst. One of the things that Daddy seemed to know a whole lot about was choosing things based on what they looked like because he warned me often against doing the same thing. Some of the stories that I could share in this chapter, I will refrain from sharing because to memorialize the personal incidents in writing that impact other people would be unfitting on my part, so I beg your forgiveness for the general broad-brush account. Though I must withhold the actual event surrounding what I am about to share, I believe that the account of Daddy's response will sufficiently do its job.

I remember a serious conversation Daddy and I had about life and a personal decision that was made that turned out badly. This time, instead of responding with one of his questions, as he was known to do, he turned the response into a parable. The parable was this. "One day, you passed by a shoe store, and there was a pair of boots in the window. The boots caught your eye, so you stopped to admire them. You didn't go in to inquire, but daily you stopped and admired those boots. They were red and fancy with pointed toes. The price tag was hidden, but you knew they had to be expensive because they were so pretty.

Those boots became your obsession until, one day, you made that life-changing decision. You went inside the store. Even though once inside, you discovered that the boots cost much more than you should pay, you bought them anyway. You looked at those boots all the way home. Finally, the occasion arose, and it was time to wear your prized possession for all the world to see. It was a little bit of a struggle to get them on your feet, but you pushed past that detail. You stepped out in style with confidence that your boots would be the best-looking thing in the room.

However, the more you strutted around that room, the more uncomfortable those boots became. Finally, those boots hurt your feet so badly that all you could think about was freeing your aching feet. When you finally limped home, you got those boots off your feet and nearly threw them back in the box." Then he added, "Just because it looks good doesn't mean it's good for you."

This parable was so impactful that even relaying the account today brings back the moment I heard it and all the reality that came with it. It is a guarantee that I had another of those watershed moments that day. Though I have missed the mark many times since then, be assured that I have become much more deliberate in looking past what appears to be good and digging deeper into the quality, the character, the motives, and even the true benefits before I "buy a pair of boots."

I am fully persuaded that though buying boots is only a simple metaphor for an incredibly important life principle, this "parable" can be translated into whatever metaphor that best describes your personal situation. This principle and all those previously shared in this simple recollection of the things my daddy said will hopefully give you insight into navigating through life with some valuable, though possibly unorthodox, tools. I wish you godspeed as you continue to traverse along and through life's adventures.

www.ingramcontent.com/pod-product-compliance
Lightning Source LLC
Chambersburg PA
CBHW051240120626
46547CB00014B/1728